THE LARK

THE
LARK

BY

Jean Anouilh

ADAPTED BY

Lillian Hellman

RANDOM HOUSE

NEW YORK

THE LARK was first presented by Kermit Bloomgarden at the Longacre Theatre, New York City, November 17, 1955, with the following cast:

WARWICK	Christopher Plummer
CAUCHON	Boris Karloff
JOAN	Julie Harris
JOAN'S FATHER	Ward Costello
JOAN'S MOTHER	Lois Holmes
JOAN'S BROTHER	John Reese
THE PROMOTER	Roger De Koven
THE INQUISITOR	Joseph Wiseman
BROTHER LADVENU	Michael Higgins
ROBERT DE BEAUDRICOURT	Theodore Bikel
AGNES SOREL	Ann Hillary
THE LITTLE QUEEN	Joan Elan
THE DAUPHIN	Paul Roebling
QUEEN YOLANDE	Rita Vale
MONSIEUR DE LA TREMOUILLE	Bruce Gordon
ARCHBISHOP OF REIMS	Richard Nicholls
CAPTAIN LA HIRE	Bruce Gordon
EXECUTIONER	Ralph Roberts
ENGLISH SOLDIER	Edward Knight
SCRIBE	Joe Bernard

LADIES OF THE COURT: Ruth Maynard, Elizabeth Lawrence.

MONKS and SOLDIERS: Michael Price, Joe Bernard, Michael Conrad, William Lennard, Milton Katselas, Edward Grower.

Directed by Joseph Anthony

Light-Setting by Jo Mielziner

Costumes by Alvin Colt

Music composed by Leonard Bernstein

SCENES

ACT ONE

The Trial

ACT TWO

The Trial

ACT ONE

ACT ONE

The music for the play was composed by Leonard Bernstein. It was sung and recorded by a group of seven men and women, without instruments, and with solos by a countertenor.

Before the curtain rises we hear the music of a psalm: the chorus is singing "Exaudi orationem meam, domine." When the curtain rises the music changes to a motet on the words "Qui tollis," from the Mass.

The Scene: Another day in the trial of JOAN. *The stage is a series of platforms, different in size and in height. The cyclorama is gray in color and projections will be thrown on it to indicate a change of scene. At this moment we see the bars of a jail as they are projected on the cyclorama.*

At rise: JOAN *is sitting on a stool.* CAUCHON *is standing downstage near* THE PROMOTER. *The* PRIESTS *are about*

3

THE LARK

to take their places on the JUDGES' *bench.* THE INQUISITOR
sits quietly on a stool near the JUDGES. JOAN's *family
stand upstage; the royal family stand in a group.* VILLAGE
WOMEN *cross the stage carrying bundles of faggots and*
ENGLISH SOLDIERS *and* GUARDS *move into place.* BEAUDRI-
COURT *and* LA HIRE *appear and take their places upstage.*
WARWICK *enters and moves through the crowd.*

WARWICK

Everybody here? Good. Let the trial begin at once.
The quicker the judgment and the burning, the better
for all of us.

CAUCHON

No, sire. The whole story must be played. Domremy,
the Voices, Chinon—

WARWICK

I am not here to watch that children's story of the warrior virgin, strong and tender, dressed in white armor,
white standard streaming in the wind. If they have time
to waste, they can make the statues that way, in days to
come. Different politics may well require different sym-
bols. We might even have to make her a monument in

4

London. Don't be shocked at that, sire. The politics of my government may well require it one day, and what's required, Englishmen supply. That's our secret, sire, and a very good one, indeed. (*Moves downstage to address the audience*) Well, let's worry about only this minute of time. I am Beauchamp, Earl of Warwick. I have a dirty virgin witch girl tucked away on a litter of straw in the depths of a prison here in Rouen. The girl has been an expensive nuisance. Your Duke of Burgundy sold her high. You like money in France, Monseigneur, all of you. That's the French secret, sire, and a very good one, indeed. (*He moves toward* JOAN) And here she is. The Maid. The famous Joan the Maid. Obviously, we paid too much. So put her on trial, and burn her, and be finished.

CAUCHON

No, sire. She must play out her whole life first. It's a short life. It won't take very long.

WARWICK

(*Moves to a stool near* CAUCHON)

If you insist. Englishmen are patient, and for the purposes of this trial I am all Englishmen. But certainly you don't intend to amuse yourselves by acting out all the

5

old battles? I would find that very disagreeable. Nobody wishes to remember defeat.

CAUCHON

No, sire. We no longer have enough men to act out the old battles. (*Turns toward* JOAN) Joan? (JOAN *turns to* CAUCHON) You may begin.

JOAN

Can I begin any place I want to?

CAUCHON

Yes.

JOAN

Then I'll start at the beginning. It's always nicer at the beginning. I'll begin with my father's house when I was very small. (*Her* MOTHER, *her* FATHER *and her* BROTHERS *appear on stage. She runs to join them*) I live here happy enough with my mother, my brothers, my father. (*We hear the music of a shepherd song and as she leaves the family group she dances her way downstage, clapping her hands to the music*) I'm in the meadow now, watching my sheep. I am not thinking of anything. It is the first time I hear the Voices. I wasn't thinking of anything. I know only that God is good and that He keeps me pure and safe in this little corner of the earth near Domremy. This one little piece of French earth that has not yet been destroyed by the English invaders. (*She makes childish thrusts with an imaginary sword, and stops suddenly as if someone has pulled her back*) Then, suddenly, someone behind me touched my shoulder. I know very well that no one is behind me. I turn and there is a great blinding light in the shadow of me. The Voice is grave and sweet and I was frightened. But I didn't tell anybody. I don't know why. Then came the second time. It was the noon Angelus. A light came over the sun and was stronger than the sun. There he was. I saw him. An angel in a beautiful clean robe that must have been ironed by somebody very careful. He had two great white wings. He didn't tell me his name that day, but later I found out he was Monseigneur the Blessed Saint Michael.

WARWICK

(*To* CAUCHON)

We know all this. Is it necessary to let her go over that nonsense again?

CAUCHON

It is necessary, sire.

JOAN

Blessed Saint Michael, excuse me, but you are in the wrong village. I am Joan, an ignorant girl, my father's daughter—(*Pauses, listens*) I can't save France. I don't even know how to ride a horse. (*Smiles*) To you people the Sire de Beaudricourt is only a country squire, but to us he is master here. He would never take me to the Dauphin, I've never even bowed to him—(*Turns to the court*) Then the Blessed Saint Michael said Saint Catherine would come along with me, and if that wasn't enough Saint Marguerite would go, too. (*She turns back as if to listen to Saint Michael*) But when the army captains lose a battle—and they lose a great many—they can go to sleep at night. I could never send men to their death. Forgive me, Blessed Saint Michael, but I must go home now—(*But she doesn't move. She is held back by a command*) Oh, Blessed Saint Michael, have pity on me. Have pity, Messire. (*The chorus sings "Alleluia, Alleluia" to the shepherd's tune. She listens, smiles, move back into the trial. Simply*) Well, he didn't. And that was the day I was saddled with France. *And* my work on the farm.

THE LARK

(THE FATHER *who has been moving about near* THE
MOTHER, *suddenly grows angry.*)

THE FATHER

What's she up to?

THE MOTHER

She's in the fields.

THE FATHER

So was I, in the fields, but I've come in. It's six o'clock!
I ask you, what's she up to?

THE BROTHER

She's dreaming under the lady tree.

THE FATHER

What's anybody doing under a tree at this hour?

THE BROTHER

You ask her. She stares straight ahead. She looks as if
she is waiting for something. It isn't the first time.

9

THE LARK

THE FATHER

(*Angrily to* THE BROTHER)

Why didn't you tell me? She is waiting for someone, not something. She has a lover.

THE MOTHER

(*Softly*)

Joan is as clean as a baby.

THE FATHER

All girls are as clean as babies until that night when they aren't any more. I'll find her and if she is with someone, I'll beat her until—

JOAN

I was with someone, but my lover had two great white wings and through the rain he came so close to me that I thought I could touch his wings. He was very worried that day, he told me so. He said the Kingdom of France was in great misery and that God said I could wait no longer. There has been a mistake, I kept saying. The Blessed Saint Michael asked me if God made mistakes. You understand that I couldn't very well say yes?

10

THE PROMOTER

Why didn't you make the Sign of the Cross?

JOAN

That question is not written in your charge against me.

THE PROMOTER

Why didn't you say to the archangel, "*Vado retro Satanas?*"

JOAN

I don't know any Latin, Messire. And *that* question is not written in your charge against me.

THE PROMOTER

Don't act the fool. The devil understands French. You could have said, "Go away, you filthy, stinking devil."

JOAN

(*Angry*)

I don't talk that way to the Blessed Saint Michael, Messire!

THE PROMOTER

The Devil told you he was Saint Michael and you were fool enough to believe him.

JOAN

I believed him. He could not have been the Devil. He was so beautiful.

THE PROMOTER

The Devil *is* beautiful!

JOAN

(Shocked)

Oh, Messire!

CAUCHON

(*To* THE PROMOTER)

These theological subtleties are far above the understanding of this poor child. You shock her without reason.

JOAN

(TO THE PROMOTER)

You've lied, Canon! I am not as educated as you are, but I know the Devil *is* ugly and everything that is beautiful is the work of God. I have no doubts. I know.

THE PROMOTER

You know nothing. Evil has a lovely face when a lovely face is needed. In real life the Devil waits for a soft, sweet night of summer. Then he comes on a gentle wind in the form of a beautiful girl with bare breasts—

CAUCHON

(*Sharply*)

Canon, let us not get mixed up in our private devils. Continue, Joan.

JOAN

(*To* THE PROMOTER)

But if the Devil is beautiful, how can we know he is the Devil?

THE PROMOTER

Go to your priest. He will tell you.

JOAN

Can't I recognize him all by myself?

THE PROMOTER

No. Certainly not. No.

JOAN

But only the rich have their priests always with them.
The poor can't be running back and forth.

THE PROMOTER

(*Angry*)

I do not like the way you speak in this court. I warn
you again—

CAUCHON

Enough, enough, Messire. Let her speak peacefully
with her Voices. There is nothing to reproach her with
so far.

JOAN

Then another time it was Saint Marguerite and Saint
Catherine who came to me. (*She turns to* THE PROMOTER)
And they, too, were beautiful.

THE PROMOTER

Were they naked?

JOAN

(*Laughs*)

Oh, Messire! Don't you think our Lord can afford to
buy clothing for His Saints?

14

CAUCHON

(*To* THE PROMOTER)

You make us all smile, Messire, with your questions. You are confusing the girl with the suggestion that good and evil is a question of what clothes are worn by what Angels and what Devils. (*Turns to* JOAN) But it is not your place to correct the venerable Canon. You forget who you are and who we are. We are your priests, your masters, and your judges. Beware of your pride, Joan.

JOAN

(*Softly*)

I know that I am proud. But I am a daughter of God. If He didn't want me to be proud, why did He send me His shining Archangel and His Saints all dressed in light? Why did He promise me that I should conquer all the men I have conquered? Why did He promise me a suit of beautiful white armor, the gift of my king? And a sword? And that I should lead brave soldiers into battle while riding a fine white horse? If He had left me alone, I would never have become proud.

CAUCHON

Take care of your words, Joan. You are accusing our Lord.

JOAN

(*Makes the Sign of the Cross*)

Oh. God forbid. I say only that His Will be done even if it means making me proud and then damning me for it. That, too, is His Right.

THE PROMOTER

(*Very angry*)

What are you saying? Could God wish to damn a human soul? How can you listen to her without shuddering, Messires? I see here the germ of a frightful heresy that could tear the Church—

(THE INQUISITOR *rises.* THE PROMOTER *stops speaking. The stage is silent.* LADVENU, *a young priest, rises and goes to* THE INQUISITOR. THE INQUISITOR *whispers to him.* LADVENU *moves to* CAUCHON, *whispers to him.*)

CAUCHON

(*Looks toward* THE INQUISITOR; *very hesitant*)

Messire—(THE INQUISITOR *stares at* CAUCHON. CAUCHON *hesitates, then turns toward* JOAN) Joan, listen well to what I must ask you. At this moment, are you in a State of Grace?

LADVENU

Messire, this is a fearful question for a simple girl who sincerely believes that God has chosen her. Do not hold her answer against her. She is in great danger and she is confused.

CAUCHON

Are you in a State of Grace?

JOAN

(As if she knew this was a dangerous question)

Which moment is that, Messire? Everything is so mixed up, I no longer know where I am. At the beginning when I heard my Voices, or at the end of the trial when I knew that my king and my friends had abandoned me? When I lost faith, when I recanted, or when, at the very last minute, I gave myself back to myself? When—

CAUCHON

(Softly, worried)

Messire demands an answer. His reasons must be grave. Joan, are you in a State of Grace?

JOAN

If I am not, God will help me in Grace. If I am, God
will keep me in Grace.

(*The* PRIESTS *murmur among themselves.* THE IN-
QUISITOR, *impassive, sits down.*)

LADVENU

(*Gently, warmly*)

Well spoken, Joan.

THE PROMOTER

(*Sharply*)

And the Devil would have the same clever answer.

WARWICK

(*To* CAUCHON, *pointing to* THE INQUISITOR)

Is that the gentleman about whom I have been told?

CAUCHON

(*Softly*)

Yes.

WARWICK

When did he arrive?

CAUCHON

Three days ago. He has wished to be alone.

WARWICK

Why was I not told of his arrival?

CAUCHON

He is one of us, sire. We do not acknowledge your authority here.

WARWICK

Only when you count our money and eat our food. Never mind, the formalities do not matter to me. But time does and I hope his presence will not add to the confusion. I am almost as bewildered as the girl. All these questions must be very interesting to you gentlemen of the Church, but if we continue at this speed we'll never get to the trial and the girl will be dead of old age. Get to the burning and be done with it.

CAUCHON

(Angry)

Sire! Who speaks of burning? We will try to save the girl—

WARWICK

Monseigneur, I allow you this charade because the object of my government is to tell the whole Christian world that the coronation of the idiot Charles was managed by a sorceress, a heretic, a mad girl, a whore campfollower. However you do that, please move with greater speed.

CAUCHON

And I remind you each day that this is a court of the Church. We are here to judge the charge of heresy. Our considerations are not yours.

WARWICK

My dear Bishop, I know that. But the fine points of ecclesiastic judgments may be a little too distinguished for my soldiers—and for the rest of the world. Propaganda is a soft weapon: hold it in your hands too long, and it will move about like a snake, and strike the other way. Whatever the girl is or has been, she must now be stripped and degraded. That is why we bought her high, and it is what we will insist upon. (*Smiles*) I'm coming to like her. I admire the way she stands up to all of you. And she rides beautifully—I've seen her. Rare to find a woman who rides that way. I'd like to have known her in other circumstances, in a pleasanter world. Hard for me to remember that she took France away from us, deprived us of our heritage. We know that God is on the side of the English. He proved himself at Agincourt. "God and my right," you know. But when this girl came along, and we began to lose, there were those who doubted our motto. That, of course, cannot be tolerated. "God and my right" is inscribed on all English armor, and we certainly have no intention of changing the armor. So get on with her story. The world will forget her soon enough. Where were we?

THE FATHER

(Comes forward)

At the moment when I find her under the lady tree. (*He goes to* JOAN) What are you doing? You were crying out to someone, but the bastard fled before I could catch him. Who was it? Who was it? Answer me. Answer me, or I'll beat you to salt mash.

JOAN

I was talking to the Blessed Saint Michael.

THE FATHER

(Hits JOAN)

That will teach you to lie to your father. You want to start whoring like the others. Well, you can tell your Blessed Saint Michael that if I catch you together I'll plunge my pitchfork into his belly and strangle you with my bare hands for the filthy rutting cat you are.

JOAN

(Softly)

Father, it was Saint Michael who was talking to me.

THE FATHER

The priest will hear about this, and from me. I'll tell him straight out that not content with running after men, you have also dared to blaspheme!

JOAN

I swear to you before God that I am telling the truth. It's been happening for a long time and always at the noon or evening Angelus. The Saints appear to me. They speak to me. They answer me when I question them. And they all say the same thing.

THE LARK

THE FATHER

Why would the Saints speak to you, idiot? I am your father, why don't they speak to me? If they had anything to say they'd talk to me.

JOAN

Father, try to understand the trouble I'm in. For three years I've refused what they ask. But I don't think I can say no much longer. I think the moment has come when I must go.

THE FATHER

For forty years I've worked myself to death to raise my children like Christians, and this is my reward. A daughter who thinks she hears Voices.

JOAN

They say I can't wait any longer—

THE FATHER

What can't wait any longer?

JOAN

They tell me France is at the last moment of danger. My Voices tell me I must save her.

THE FATHER

You?—You? You are crazy. Crazy. You are a fool! A fool and a crazy girl.

JOAN

I must do what my Voices tell me. I will go to the Sire de Beaudricourt and ask him to give me an armed escort to the Dauphin at Chinon. I'll talk to the Dauphin and make him fight. Then I will take the army to Orléans and we'll push the English into the sea.

THE FATHER

For ten years I have dreamed that you would disgrace us with men. Do you think I raised you, sacrificed everything for you, to have you run off to live with soldiers? I knew what you would be. But you won't—I'll kill you first.

(*He begins to beat her and to kick her.*)

JOAN

(*Screams*)

Stop! Stop! Oh, Father, stop!

THE LARK

LADVENU

(*Rises, horrified*)

Stop him. Stop him. He's hurting her.

CAUCHON

We cannot, Brother Ladvenu. We do not know Joan. You forget that we first meet her at the trial. We can only play our roles, good or bad, just as they were, each in his turn. And we will hurt her far more than he does. You know that. (*Turns to* WARWICK) Ugly, isn't it, this family scene?

WARWICK

Why? In England we are in favor of strong punishment for children. It makes character. I was half beaten to death as a boy, but I am in excellent health.

THE FATHER

(*He looks down at* JOAN *who has fallen at his feet*)

Crazy little whore. Do you still want to save France? (*Then, shamefaced, he turns to the* JUDGES) Well, messieurs, what would you have done in my place if your daughter had been like that?

THE LARK

If we had known about this girl from the very beginning, we could have reached an agreement with her
father. We tell people that our intelligence service is remarkable and we say it so often that everybody believes
us. It should be their business not only to tell us what is
happening, but what might happen. When a country virgin talked about saving France, I should have known
about it. I tell myself now I would not have laughed.

(THE MOTHER *comes forward. She bends over*
JOAN.)

THE FATHER
(*To* THE MOTHER)

The next time your daughter talks of running after soldiers, I'll put her in the river and with my own hands
I'll hold her under.

(THE MOTHER *takes* JOAN *in her arms*)

THE MOTHER

He hurt you bad.

JOAN

Yes.

26

THE LARK

THE MOTHER

(*Softly*)

He's your father.

JOAN

Yes. He is my father. Oh, Mama, somebody must understand. I can't do it alone.

THE MOTHER

Lean against me. You're big now. I can hardly hold
you in my arms. Joan, your father is a good and honest
man but—(*She whispers in* JOAN's *ear*) I've saved a little
from the house money. If you'd like one, I'll buy you a
broidered kerchief at the very next fair.

JOAN

I don't need a kerchief. I won't ever be pretty, Mama.

THE MOTHER

We're all a little wild when we're young. Who is it,
Joan? Don't have secrets from me. Is he from our village?

27

JOAN

I don't want to marry, Mama. That isn't what I mean.

THE MOTHER

Then what do you mean?

JOAN

Blessed Saint Michael says that I must put on man's clothes. He says that I must save France.

THE MOTHER

Joan, I speak to you in kindness, but I forbid you to tell me such nonsense. A man's clothes! I should just like to see you try it.

JOAN

But I'll have to, Mama, if I'm to ride horse with my soldiers. Saint Michael makes good sense.

THE MOTHER

Your soldiers? Your soldiers? You bad girl! I'd rather see you dead first. Now I'm talking like your father, and that I never want to do. (*She begins to cry*) Running after soldiers! What have I done to deserve a daughter like this? You will kill me.

28

JOAN

No, Mama, no. (*She cries out as her* MOTHER *moves off*) Monseigneur Saint Michael. It cannot be done. No-body will ever understand. It is better for me to say no right now. (*Pauses, listens*) Then Saint Michael's voice grew soft, the way it does when he is angry. And he said that I must take the first step. He said that God trusted me and if a mountain of ice did rise ahead of me it was only because God was busy and trusted me to climb the mountain even if I tore my hands and broke my legs, and my face might run with blood—(*After a second, slowly, carefully*) Then I said that I would go. I said that I would go that day.

> (JOAN'S BROTHER *comes forward and stands looking at her.*)

THE BROTHER

You haven't got the sense you were born with. If you give me something next time, I won't tell Papa I saw you with your lover.

JOAN

So it was you, you pig, you told them? Here's what I'll give you this time—(*She slaps him*) And the next time—(*She slaps him again, and begins to chase him. He runs from her*) and the time after that. (JOAN'S *voice changes and she moves slowly about not concerned with him any longer but speaking into space*) And so I went to my uncle Durand. And my uncle Durand went to the seigneur of the manor. And I walked a long way west and a little way south and there was the night I was shivering with rain—or with fear—and the day I was shivering with sun—or with fear—and then I walked to the west again and east. I was on my way to the first fool I had to deal with. And I had plenty of them to deal with.

(*She moves upstage, bumps into two* SOLDIERS *as* BEAUDRICOURT *comes on stage.*)

BEAUDRICOURT

What is it? What's the matter? What does she want? What's the matter with these crazy fools? (*He grabs* JOAN *and shakes her*) What's the matter with you, young woman? You've been carrying on like a bad girl. I've heard about you standing outside the doors ragging at the sentries until they fall asleep.

JOAN

(*He holds her up. She dangles in front of his face*)
I want a horse. I want the dress of a man. I want an armed escort. You will give them orders to take me to Chinon to see the Dauphin.

BEAUDRICOURT

Of course. And I will also kick you in the place where it will do the most good.

JOAN

Kicks, blows. Whichever you like best. I'm used to them by now. I want a horse. I want the dress of a man. I want an armed escort.

BEAUDRICOURT

That's a new idea—a horse. You know who I am and what I usually want? Did the village girls tell you? When they come to ask a favor it usually has to do with a father or a brother who has poached my land. If the girl is pretty, I have a good heart, and we both pitch in. If the girl is ugly, well, usually I have a good heart, too, but not so good as the other way. I am known in this land for good-heartedness. But a horse is a nasty kind of bargain.

JOAN

I have been sent by Blessed Saint Michael.

BEAUDRICOURT

(*Puts her down hurriedly, makes the Sign of the Cross*)
Don't mix the Saints up in this kind of thing. That talk

was good enough to get you past the sentries, but it's not good enough to get you a horse. A horse costs more than a woman. You're a country girl. You ought to know that. Are you a virgin?

JOAN

Yes, sire.

BEAUDRICOURT

Well, maybe we'll talk about a small horse. You have lovely eyes.

JOAN

I want more than a horse, sire.

BEAUDRICOURT

(*Laughs*)

You're greedy. But I like that sometimes. There are fools who get angry when the girl wants too much. But I say good things should cost a lot. That pleases me in a girl. You understand what I mean?

JOAN

No, sire.

BEAUDRICOURT

That's good. I don't like clear-thinking women in bed.
Not in my bed. You understand what I mean?

JOAN

No, sire.

BEAUDRICOURT

Well, I don't like idiots, either. What is it you're up to?
What else besides a horse?

JOAN

Just as I said before, sire. An armed escort as far as
Chinon.

BEAUDRICOURT

Stop that crazy talk. I'm the master here. I can send
you back where you came from with no better present
than the lashes of a whip. I told you I like a girl to come
high, but if she costs too much the opposite effect sets in
—and I can't—well, I can't. You understand what I
mean? (*Suddenly*) Why do you want to go to Chinon?

JOAN

As I said before, sire, I wish to find Monseigneur the
Dauphin.

33

BEAUDRICOURT

Well, you *are* on a high road. Why not the Duke of Burgundy while you're at it? He's more powerful, and he likes the girls. But not our Dauphin. He runs from war and women. An hour with either would kill him. Why do you want to see such a fellow?

JOAN

I want an army, Messire. An army to march upon Orléans.

BEAUDRICOURT

If you're crazy, forget about me. (*Shouting*) Boudousse. Boudousse. (*A* SOLDIER *comes forward*) Throw some cold water on this girl and send her back to her father. Don't beat her. It's bad luck to beat a crazy woman.

JOAN

You won't beat me. You're a kind man, Messire. Very kind.

BEAUDRICOURT

Sometimes yes, sometimes no. But I don't like virgins whose heads come off at night—

34

JOAN

And you're very intelligent, which is sometimes even better than being kind. But when a man is intelligent *and* kind, then that's the very best combination on God's fine earth.

BEAUDRICOURT

(*He waves the* GUARD *away*)
You're a strange girl. Want a little wine? Why do you think I'm intelligent?

JOAN

It shows in your face. You're handsome, Messire.

BEAUDRICOURT

Twenty years ago, I wouldn't have said no. I married two rich widows, God bless me. But not now. Of course, I've tried not to get old too fast, and there are men who get better looking with age—(*Smiles*) You know, it's very comic to be talking like this with a shepherd girl who drops out of the sky one bright morning. I am bored here. My officers are animals. I have nobody to talk to. I like a little philosophy now and then. I should like to know from your mouth what connection you see between

35

beauty and intelligence? Usually people say that handsome men are stupid.

JOAN

Hunchbacks talk that way, and people with long noses,
or those who will die of a bitter egg that grows in their
head. God has the power to create a perfect man—(*She
smiles at him*) And sometimes He uses His power.

BEAUDRICOURT

Well, you can look at it that way, of course. But you
take me, for example. No, I'm not ugly, but sometimes I
wonder if I'm intelligent. No, no, don't protest. I tell you
there are times when I have problems that seem too
much for me. They ask me to decide something, a tactical
or administrative point. Then, all of a sudden, I don't
know why, my head acts like it's gone some place else,
and I don't even understand the words people are saying. Isn't that strange? (*After a second*) But I never show
it. I roar out an order whatever happens. That's the main
thing in an army. Make a decision, good or bad, just *make*
it. Things will turn out almost the same, anyway. (*Softly,
as if to himself*) Still, I wish I could have done better.
This is a small village to die away your life. (*Points*

outside) They think I'm a great man, but they never saw anybody else. Like every other man, I wanted to be brilliant and remarkable, but I end up hanging a few poor bastards who deserted from a broken army. I wanted to shake a nation—Ah, well. (*Looks at her*) Why do I tell you all this? You can't help me, and you're crazy.

JOAN

They told me you would speak this way.

BEAUDRICOURT

They told you?

JOAN

Listen to me, nice, good Robert, and don't shout any more. It's useless. I'm about to say something very important. You will be brilliant and remarkable. You will shake a nation because *I* will do it for you. Your name will go far outside this village—

BEAUDRICOURT

(*Puts his arms around her*)

What are you talking about?

37

JOAN

(*She pulls away from him*)

Robert, don't think any more about my being a girl. That just confuses everything. You'll find plenty of girls who are prettier and will give more pleasure—(*Softly*) and will not ask as much. You don't want me.

BEAUDRICOURT

Well, I don't know. You're all right.

JOAN

(*Sharply*)

If you want me to help you, then help me. When I say the truth say it with me.

BEAUDRICOURT

(*Politely*)

But you're a pleasant-looking girl, and it's nice weather, and . . . (*Laughs*) No, I don't want you any more than that.

JOAN

Good. Now that we have got that out of the way, let's pretend that you've given me the clothes of a boy and we're sitting here like two comrades talking good sense.

THE LARK

BEAUDRICOURT

(*Fills a glass*)

All right. Have a little wine.

JOAN

(*Drinks her wine*)

Kind, sweet Robert. Great things are about to begin for you. (*As he starts to speak*) No, no. Listen. The English are everywhere, and everywhere they are our masters. Brittany and Anjou will go next. The English wait only to see which one will pay the higher tribute money. The Duke of Burgundy signs a bitter treaty and the English give him the Order of the Golden Fleece. They invented just such medals for foreign traitors. Our little monkey Dauphin Charles sits with his court in Bourges, shaking and jibbering. He knows nothing, his court knows nothing, and all falls to pieces around him. You know that. You know our army, our good army of brave boys, is tired and sick. They believe the English will always be stronger and that there's no sense to it any more. When an army thinks that way, the end is near. The Bastard Dunois is a good captain and intelligent. So intelligent that nobody will listen to him. So he forgets that he should be leading an army and drowns himself in wine,

39

and tells stories of past battles to his whores. I'll put a
stop to that, you can be sure—

BEAUDRICOURT

(*Softly*)

You'll put a stop to—

JOAN

Our best soldiers are like angry bulls. They always
want to attack, to act fine for the history books. They are
great champions of individual bravery. But they don't
know how to use their cannon and they get people killed
for nothing. That's what they did at Agincourt. Ah, when
it comes to dying, they're all ready to volunteer. But
what good is it to die? You think just as I do, my dear
Robert: war isn't a tournament for fancy gentlemen. You
must be smart to win a war. You must think, and be
smart. (*Quickly*) But you who are so intelligent, knew all
that when you were born.

BEAUDRICOURT

I've always said it. I've always said that nobody thinks
any more. I used to be a thinker, but nobody paid any attention.

JOAN

They will, they will. Because you have just had an idea that will probably save all of us.

BEAUDRICOURT

I've had an idea?

JOAN

Well, you are about to have it. But don't let anything get in its way. Please sit quiet and don't, well, just—(*As he is about to move she holds him down*) You are the only man in France who at this minute can see the future. Sit still.

BEAUDRICOURT

What is it that I see?

JOAN

You know your soldiers. You know they will leave you soon. You know that to keep them you must give them faith. You have nothing else to give them now. A little bread, a little faith—good simple things to fight with.

BEAUDRICOURT

It's too late—

JOAN

A girl comes before you. Saint Michael and Saint Catherine and Saint Marguerite have told her to come. You will say it's not true. But I believe it *is* true, and that's what matters. A farm girl who says that God is on her side. You can't prove He isn't. You can't. Try it and see. The girl came a long, hard way, she got so far as you, and she has convinced you. Yes, I have. I have convinced you. And why have I convinced so intelligent a man? Because I tell the truth, and it takes a smart head to know the truth.

BEAUDRICOURT

Where is this idea you said I had?

JOAN

Coming, coming just this minute. You are saying to yourself, if she convinced me, why shouldn't she convince the Dauphin and Dunois and the Archbishop? After all they're only men like me, although a good deal less intelligent. (*Very fast*) All right, that's settled. But now you're saying to yourself when it comes to dying, soldiers are very intelligent, and so she'll have a harder time with them. No, she won't. She will say English heads are like all others: hit them hard enough, at the right time, and we'll march over them to Orléans. They need faith, your soldiers. They need somebody who believes it to say that God is on their side. Everybody says things like that. But *I* believe it—and that's the difference. Our soldiers will fight again, you know it, and because you know it you are the most remarkable man in France.

BEAUDRICOURT

You think so?

JOAN

The whole world will think so. But you must move fast. Like all great political men you are a realist. At this minute you are saying to yourself, "If the troops will believe this girl has come from God, what difference does it make whether she has or not? I will send her to Bourges tomorrow with the courier."

BEAUDRICOURT

The courier does go tomorrow. How did you know that? He goes with a secret packet—

43

JOAN

(*Laughs, delighted*)

Give me six good soldiers and a fine white horse. I want a *white* horse, please. I will do the rest. But give me a quiet white horse because I don't know how to ride.

BEAUDRICOURT

(*Laughs*)

You'll break your neck.

JOAN

It's up to Blessed Saint Michael to keep me in the saddle. (*He laughs. She doesn't like his laughter*) I will make you a bet, Robert. I'll bet you a man's dress that if you will have two horses brought now, and we both ride at a gallop, I won't fall off. If I stay on, then will you believe in me? All right?

BEAUDRICOURT

(*Laughs*)

All this thinking makes a man weary. I had other plans for this afternoon, as I told you, but any kind of exercise is good for me. Come on.

44

(*He exits.* JOAN, *smiling, looks toward Heaven. Then she runs after* BEAUDRICOURT. *But she is stopped by a* SOLDIER *and suddenly realizes she is back in the trial. She sits quietly as the lights fade out on the* BEAUDRICOURT *scene.*)

WARWICK

She made that idiot believe he wasn't an idiot.

CAUCHON

It was a man-woman scene, a little coarse for my taste.

WARWICK

Coarse for *your* taste? The trick of making him believe what she put into his head is exactly what I do in my trade and what you do in yours. (*Suddenly*) Speaking of your trade, sire, forgive a brutal question but, just between ourselves, do you really have the faith?

CAUCHON

(*Simply*)

As a child has it. And that is why my judges and I will try to save Joan. To the bitter end we will try to save her. Our honor demands that—(WARWICK *turns away.* CAU-

45

CHON, *sharply*) You think of us as collaborators and therefore without honor. We believed that collaboration with you was the only reasonable solution—

WARWICK

And so it was. But when you say reasonable solution it is often more honorable to omit the word honor.

CAUCHON

(*Softly*)

I say honor. Our poor honor, the little that was left us, demanded that we fight for our beliefs.

WARWICK

While you lived on English money—

CAUCHON

Yes. And while eight hundred of your soldiers were at our gates. It was easy for free men to call us traitors, but we lived in occupied territory, dependent upon the will of your king to kill us or to feed us. We were men, and we wanted to live; we were priests, and we wanted to save Joan. Like most other men, we wanted everything. We played a shameful role.

WARWICK

Shameful? I don't know. You might have played a nobler part, perhaps, if you had decided to be martyrs and fight against us. My eight hundred men were quite ready to help.

CAUCHON

We had good reason to know about your soldiers. I remember no day without insults and threats. And yet we stood against you. Nine long months before we agreed to hand over a girl who had been deserted by everybody but us. They can call us barbarians, but for all their noble principles I believe they would have surrendered her before we did.

WARWICK

You could have given us the girl on the first day. Nine long months of endless what?

CAUCHON

It was hard for us. God had been silent since Joan's arrest. He had not spoken to her or to us. Therefore, we had to do without his counsel. We were here to defend the House of God. During our years in the seminaries we learned how to defend it. Joan had no training in our

47

seminaries and yet, abandoned, she defended God's House in her own way. Defended it with that strange conflict of insolence and humility, worldly sense and un-worldly grandeur. (*Softly*) The piety was so simple and sweet—to the last moment of the last flame. We did not understand her in those days. We covered our eyes like old, fighting, childish men, and turned away so that we could not hear the cries of anguish. She was all alone at the end. God had not come to her. That is a terrible time for a religious nature, sire, and brings doubt and despair unknown to others. (CAUCHON *rises and turns away*) But it is then and there that some men raise their heads, and when they do, it is a noble sight.

WARWICK

Yes, it is. But as a man of politics, I cannot afford the doctrine of man's individual magnificence. I might meet another man who felt the same way. And he might express his individual magnificence by cutting off *my* head.

CAUCHON

(*Softly, as if he hadn't heard* WARWICK)
Sometimes, to console myself, I remember how beautiful were all those old priests who tried to protect the child, to save her from what can never now be mended—

WARWICK

Oh, you speak in large words, sire. Political language
has no such words as "never now be mended." I have told
you that the time will come when we will raise her a
statue in London.

CAUCHON

And the time will come when our names will be known
only for what we did to her; when men, forgiving their
own sins, but angry with ours, will speak our names in a
curse—

(*The lights dim on* WARWICK *and* CAUCHON *and we
hear the music of a court song. A throne is
brought on stage and as the lights come up slowly on* THE DAUPHIN'S *Court, the cyclorama re-
flects the royal fleur-de-lis.* THE DAUPHIN, CHARLES,
is lolling about on his throne playing at bilboquet.
AGNES SOREL *and* THE LITTLE QUEEN *are practicing
a new dance.* YOLANDE *is moving about. Four*
COURTIERS *are playing at cards.*)

THE LITTLE QUEEN

(*She is having a hard time learning the dance steps*)
It's very hard.

AGNES

Everything is very hard for you, dear.

THE LITTLE QUEEN

(*As they pass* CHARLES)

It's a new dance. Very fashionable. Influenced by the Orient, they say.

AGNES

(*To* CHARLES)

Come. We'll teach you.

CHARLES

I won't be going to the ball.

AGNES

Well, *we* will be going. And we must dance better than anybody else and look better than anybody else. (*Stops, to* CHARLES, *points to her headdress*) And I'm not going in this old thing. I'm your mistress. Have a little pride. A mistress must be better dressed than anybody. You know that.

THE LARK

THE LITTLE QUEEN

And so must wives. I mean better dressed than other wives. The Queen of France in last year's shoddy. What do you think they will say, Charles?

CHARLES

They will say that poor little Queen married a king who hasn't a sou. They will be wrong. I have a sou.
(*He throws a coin in the air. It falls and he begins to scramble on the floor for it.*)

THE LITTLE QUEEN

I can hear them all the way to London. The Duchess of Bedford and the Duchess of Gloucester—
(CHARLES, *on the floor, is about to find his sou as the* ARCHBISHOP *and* LA TREMOUILLE *come in.* CHARLES *jumps back in fear.*)

LA TREMOUILLE

(*To* CHARLES)
You grow more like your father each day.

ARCHBISHOP

But his father had the decency to take to his bed.

CHARLES

Which father?

LA TREMOUILLE

You act so strangely, sire, that even I, who knew your mother, am convinced you are legitimate. (*Angrily, to* CHARLES *who is still on the floor*) Move. Move.

THE LITTLE QUEEN

Oh, please don't speak to him that way, Monsieur de la Tremouille.

ARCHBISHOP

(*Who has been glaring at the dancers*)
You believe this is the proper time for dancing?

THE LITTLE QUEEN

But if the English take us prisoner, we have to know a little something. We can't disgrace our country—
(LA TREMOUILLE *stares at her, exits.*)

YOLANDE

What harm do they do, sire? They are young—and there isn't much ahead for them.

ARCHBISHOP

There isn't much ahead for any of us.
(*He moves off.*)

YOLANDE

Please get up, Charles. It is a sad thing to see you so frightened by so many men.

CHARLES

And why shouldn't I be frightened of La Tremouille and the Archbishop? I have been all my life. They could order every soldier in the place to cut me up and eat me.

AGNES

They're cheats, every woman in England. We set the styles—and they send spies to steal the latest models. But, fortunately, they're so ugly that nothing looks very well— (*Admires her own feet and hands*) with cows for feet and pigs for hands. We want new headdresses. Are you the King of France or aren't you?

CHARLES

I don't know if I am. Nobody knows. I told you all about that the first night you came to bed.

AGNES

The new headdress is two feet tall and has two horns coming from the side—

CHARLES

Sounds like a man. A very small married man.

THE LITTLE QUEEN

And they have a drape at the back—they will cause a revolution, Charles.

AGNES

The English ladies—the mistresses, I mean, of course— won't be able to sleep when they see us. And if they can't sleep neither will the Dukes. And if the Dukes can't sleep they won't feel well and they won't have time to march on us—

CHARLES

They won't march on us. Nobody wants this dull town. They're already in Orléans. So there isn't much sense counterattacking with a headdress.

THE LITTLE QUEEN

Oh, Charles, one has to have a little pleasure in life. And Mama—(*Pointing to* YOLANDE) and the Archbishop and La Tremouille, and all the wise people, tell us that the end is here, anyway, and this will be the last state ball—

CHARLES

How much do they cost?

AGNES

I flirted with the man—(*Hastily*) in a nice way—and he's going to let us have them for six thousand francs.

CHARLES

Where would I get six thousand francs, you little idiot?

THE LITTLE QUEEN

Twelve thousand francs, Charles. I'm here.

CHARLES

That's enough to pay Dunois' army the six months' wages that I owe them. You are dreaming, my kittens. My dear mother-in-law, please speak to these children.

YOLANDE

No. I wish to speak to you.

CHARLES

For two days you've been following me about looking the way good women always look when they're about to give a lecture.

YOLANDE

Have I ever spoken against your interests? Have I ever shown myself concerned with anything but your welfare? I am the mother of your Queen, but I brought Agnes to you when I realized she would do you good.

THE LITTLE QUEEN

Please, Mama, don't brag about it.

YOLANDE

My child, Agnes is a charming girl and she knows her place. It was important that Charles make up his mind to become a man, and if he was to become a man he had to have a woman.

THE LITTLE QUEEN

I am a woman and his wife in the bargain.

YOLANDE

You are my dear little girl and I don't want to hurt you, but you're not very much of a woman. I know because I was just like you. I was honest and sensible, and that was all. Be the Queen to your Charles, keep his house, give him a Dauphin. But leave the rest to others. Love is not a business for honest women. We're no good at it. Charles is more virile since he knows Agnes. (*Worried*) You are more virile, aren't you, Charles?

AGNES

(*Too firmly*)

Yes, indeed.

YOLANDE

I hope so. He doesn't act it with the Archbishop or La Tremouille.

AGNES

Things like that take a while. But he's much more virile. Doesn't read so much any more. (*To* CHARLES) And since it's all due to me the very least you can do is to give me the headdress. And one for the little Queen. (CHARLES *doesn't answer*) I feel ill. And if I feel ill it will certainly be for a whole week. And you'll be very bored without me. (*Eagerly, as she sees his face*) Sign a Treasury Bond and we'll worry afterwards. (*He nods. She turns to* THE LITTLE QUEEN) Come, my little Majesty. The pink one

57

for you, the green one for me. (*To* CHARLES, *as they exit*)
We'll make fools of those London ladies, you'll see. It'll
be a great victory for France.

CHARLES

(*To* YOLANDE)

A great victory for France. She talks like an army
captain. I'm sick of such talk. France will be victorious,
you'll be a great king—all the people who have wanted
to make a king out of me. Even Agnes. She practices in
bed. That's very funny. I must tell you about it some
day. I am a poor frightened nothing with a lost kingdom
and a broken army. When will they understand that?

YOLANDE

I understand it, Charles.

CHARLES

(*Softly, taken aback*)

Do you? You've never said that before.

YOLANDE

I say it now because I want you to see this girl. For
three days I have had her brought here, waiting for you—

CHARLES

I am ridiculous enough without playing games with village louts who come to me on clouds carrying a basket of dreams.

YOLANDE

There is something strange about this girl, something remarkable. Or so everybody thinks, and that's what matters.

CHARLES

You know La Tremouille would never allow me to see the girl.

YOLANDE

Why not? It is time they understood that a peasant at their council table might do a little good. A measure of common sense from humble people might bring us all—

CHARLES

(*Sharply*)

To ruin. Men of the people have been at council tables, have become kings, and it was a time of massacre and mistake. At least I'm harmless. The day

59

may come when Frenchmen will regret their little Charles. At least, I have no large ideas about how to organize happiness and death.

(*He throws his ball in the air.*)

YOLANDE

Please stop playing at bilboquet, Charles.

CHARLES

Let me alone. I like this game. When I miss the cup, the ball only falls on my nose, and that hurts nobody but me. But if I sit straight on the throne with the ball in one hand and the stick in the other, I might start taking myself seriously. Then the ball will fall on the nose of France, and the nose of France won't like it.

(*The* ARCHBISHOP *and* LA TREMOUILLE *enter.*)

LA TREMOUILLE

We have a new miracle every day. The girl walked to the village church to say her prayers. A drunken soldier yelled an insult at her. "You are wrong to curse," she said, "You will soon appear before our Lord." An hour later the soldier fell into a well and was drowned. The stumbling of a drunkard has turned the town into a roaring holiday. They are marching here now, shouting that God commands you to receive this girl.

CHARLES

He hasn't said a word to me.

LA TREMOUILLE

The day God speaks to you, sire, I will turn infidel.

ARCHBISHOP
(Very angry)

Put up that toy, your majesty. You will have the rest of your life to devote to it.

LA TREMOUILLE

Get ready to leave here.

CHARLES

Where will I go? Where will you go? To the English?

ARCHBISHOP

Even from you, sire, we will not accept such words.
(*As* LA TREMOUILLE *angrily advances on* CHARLES, YOLANDE *moves between them.*)

YOLANDE

(*To* ARCHBISHOP)

Allow him to see the girl.

ARCHBISHOP

And throw open the palace to every charlatan, every bone setter, every faith healer in the land?

LA TREMOUILLE

What difference does it make any more? We have come to the end of our rope.

YOLANDE

If he sees the girl, it will give the people hope for a few days.

CHARLES

Oh, I am tired of hearing about the girl. Bring her in and have it ended. Maybe she has a little money and can play cards.

YOLANDE

(*To* LA TREMOUILLE)

We have nothing to lose, sire—

THE LARK

LA TREMOUILLE

When you deal with God you risk losing everything. If He has really sent this girl then He has decided to concern Himself with us. In that case, we are in even worse trouble than we thought. People who govern states should not attract God's attention. They should make themselves very small and pray that they will go unnoticed.

(JOAN *comes in. She stands small and frightened, staring at* CHARLES, *bowing respectfully to the* ARCHBISHOP. *As she moves toward the throne, one of the* COURTIERS *laughs.* JOAN *turns to stare, and the* COURTIER *draws back as if he is frightened.*)

CHARLES

What do you want? I'm a very busy man. It's time for my milk.

JOAN

(*Bows before him*)

I am Joan the Maid. The King of Heaven has sent me here. I am to take you to Reims and have you anointed and crowned King of France.

CHARLES

My. Well, that is splended, mademoiselle, but Reims is in the hands of the English, as far as I know. How shall we get there?

JOAN

We will fight our way there, noble Dauphin. First, we will take Orléans and then we will walk to Reims.

LA TREMOUILLE

I am commander of the army, madame. We have not been able to take Orléans.

JOAN

(Carefully)

I will do it, sire. With the help of our Lord God who is my only commander.

LA TREMOUILLE

When did Orléans come to God's attention?

JOAN

I do not know the hour, but I know that he wishes us to take the city. After that, we will push the English into the sea.

LA TREMOUILLE

Is the Lord in such bad shape that he needs you to do his errands?

JOAN

He has said that he needs me.

ARCHBISHOP

Young woman—(JOAN *kneels and kisses the hem of his robe*) If God wishes to save the Kingdom of France he has no need of armies.

JOAN

Monseigneur, God doesn't want a lazy Kingdom of France. We must put up a good fight and then He will give us victory.

ARCHBISHOP

(*To* CHARLES)

The replies of this girl are, indeed, interesting and make a certain amount of good sense. But this is a delicate matter: a commission of learned doctors will now examine her. We will review their findings in council—

THE LARK

LA TREMOUILLE

(*To* CHARLES)

And will keep you informed of our decision. Go back to your book. She will not disturb you any more today. Come, Madame Henriette—

JOAN

My name is Joan.

LA TREMOUILLE

Forgive me. The last quack was called Henriette.

ARCHBISHOP

Come, my child—

CHARLES

No! (*He motions to* JOAN) You. Don't move. (*He turns toward* LA TREMOUILLE, *standing straight and stiff and holding* JOAN's *hand to give himself courage*) Leave me alone with her. (*Giggles*) Your King commands you. (LA TREMOUILLE *and the* ARCHBISHOP *bow and leave.* CHARLES *holds his noble pose for an instant, then bursts into laughter*) And they went. It's the first time they ever obeyed me. (*Very worried*) You haven't come here to kill me?

(*She smiles*) No. No, of course not. You have an honest face. I've lived so long with those pirates that I've almost forgotten what an honest face looks like. Are there other people who have honest faces?

JOAN
(*Gravely*)

Many, sire.

CHARLES

I never see them. Brutes and whores, that's all I ever see. And the little Queen. She's nice, but she's stupid. And Agnes. She's not stupid—and she's not nice. (*He climbs on his throne, hangs his feet over one of the arms and sighs*) All right. Start boring me. Tell me that I ought to be a great King.

JOAN
(*Softly*)

Yes, Charles.

CHARLES

Listen. If you want to make an impression on the Archbishop and the council, we'll have to stay in this room for at least an hour. If you talk to me of God and the Kingdom of France, I'll never live through the hour. Let's do something else. Do you know how to play at cards?

JOAN

I don't know what it is.

CHARLES

It is a nice game invented to amuse my Papa when he was ill. I'll teach you. (*He begins to hunt for the cards*) I hope they haven't stolen them. They steal everything from me around here and cards are expensive. Only the wealthiest princes can have them. I got mine from Papa. I'll never have the price of another pack. If those pigs have stolen them—No. Here they are. (*He finds them in his pocket*) My Papa was crazy. Went crazy young—in his thirties. Did you know that? Sometimes I am glad I am a bastard. At least I don't have to be so frightened of going crazy. Then sometimes I wish I were his son and knew that I was meant to be a king. It's confusing.

JOAN

Of the two, which would you prefer?

CHARLES

Well, on the days when I have a little courage, I'd risk going crazy. But on the days when I haven't any courage—that's from Sunday to Saturday—I would rather let everything go to hell and live in peace in some foreign land on whatever little money I have left.

JOAN

Today, Charles, is this one of the days when you have courage?

CHARLES

Today? (*He thinks a minute*) Yes, it seems to me I have a little bit today. Not much, but a little bit. I was sharp with the Archbishop, and—

JOAN

You will have courage every day. Beginning now.

CHARLES

You have a charm in a bottle or a basket?

JOAN

I have a charm.

69

CHARLES

You are a witch? You can tell me, you know, because I don't care. I swear to you that I won't repeat it. I have a horror of people being tortured. A long time ago, they made me witness the burning of a heretic at the stake. I vomited all night long.

JOAN

I am not a witch. But I have a charm.

CHARLES

Sell it to me without telling the others.

JOAN

I will give it to you, Charles. For nothing.

CHARLES

Then I don't want it. What you get free costs too much. (*He shuffles the cards*) I act like a fool so that people will let me alone. My Papa was so crazy they think I am, too. He was very crazy, did all kinds of strange things, some of them very funny. One day he thought it would be nice to have a great funeral, but nobody happened to die just then so he decided to bury a man who'd been dead four years. It cost a fortune to dig him out and put him back, but it was fun. (*He laughs merrily, catches himself, stares at* JOAN) But don't think you can catch me too easily. I know a little about the world.

JOAN

You know too much. You are too smart.

CHARLES

Yes. Because I must defend myself against these cut-throats. They've got large bones, I've got puny sticks. But my head's harder than theirs and I've clung to my throne by using it.

JOAN

(*Gently*)

I would like to defend you against them, Charles. I would give my life to do it.

CHARLES

Do you mean that?

JOAN

Yes. And I'm not afraid of anything.

CHARLES

You're lucky. Or you're a liar. Sit down and I'll teach you to play.

JOAN

All right. You teach me this game and I'll teach you another game.

CHARLES

What game do you know?

JOAN

How not to be too smart. (*Softly*) And how not to be afraid.

CHARLES

(*Laughs*)

You'll be here a lifetime, my girl. Now. See these cards? They have pictures painted on them. Kings, queens and knaves, just as in real life. Now which would you say was the most powerful, which one could take all the rest?

JOAN

The king.

72

CHARLES

Well, you're wrong. This large heart can take the king.
It can put him to rout, break his heart, win all his money.
This card is called—

JOAN

I know. It is called God. Because God is more powerful
than kings.

CHARLES

Oh, leave God alone for a minute. It's called the ace.
Are you running this game? God this and God that. You
talk as if you dined with Him last night. Didn't anybody
tell you that the English also say their prayers to God?
Every man thinks God is on his side. The rich and powerful know He is. But we're not rich and powerful, you
and I—and France.

JOAN

That isn't what God cares about. He is angry with us
because we have no courage left. God doesn't like
frightened people.

CHARLES

Then He certainly doesn't like me. And if He doesn't
like me, why should I like Him? He could have given me
courage. I wanted it.

JOAN

(*Sharply*)

Is God your nurse? Couldn't you have tried to do a little better? Even with those legs.

CHARLES

I am sorry to know that my legs have already come to your attention. It's because of my legs that Agnes can never really love me. That's sad, isn't it?

JOAN

No.

CHARLES

Why not?

JOAN

Because your head is ugly, too, and you can't be sad about everything. But what's inside your head isn't ugly, because God gave you sense. And what do you do with it? Play cards. Bounce a ball in the air. Play baby tricks with the Archbishop and act the fool for all to see. You have a son. But what have you made for him? Nothing.

And when he's grown he, too, will have a right to say, "God didn't like me, so why should I like Him?" But when he says God he will mean you because every son thinks his father is God. And when he's old enough to know that, he will hate you for what you didn't give him.

CHARLES

Give him? What can I give him? I'm glad to be alive. I've told you the truth: I am afraid. I've always been and I always will be.

JOAN

And now I'll tell you the truth: I am also afraid. (*With force*) And why not? Only the stupid are not afraid. What is the matter with you? Don't you understand that it was far more dangerous for me to get here than it is for you to build a kingdom? I've been in danger every minute of the way, and every minute of the way I was frightened. I don't want to be beaten, I don't want pain, I don't want to die. I am scared.

CHARLES

(*Softly*)

What do you do when you get scared?

75

JOAN

Act as if I wasn't. It's that simple. Try it. Say to yourself, yes, I am afraid. But it's nobody else's business, so go on, go on. And you do go on.

CHARLES

(*Softly*)

Where do you go?

JOAN

(*Slowly, carefully*)

To the English, outside Orléans. And when you get there and see the cannon and the archers, and you know you are outnumbered, you will say to yourself, all right, they are stronger than I am, and that frightens me, as well it should. But I'll march right through because I had sense enough to get frightened first.

CHARLES

March through a stronger army? That can't be done.

JOAN

Yes it can. If you have sense and courage. Do you want to know what happened in my village last year?

76

They tell the story as a miracle now but it wasn't. The Bouchon boy went hunting. He's the best poacher in our village, and this day he was poaching on the master's grounds. The master kept a famous dog, trained to kill, and the dog found the Bouchon boy. The boy was caught and death faced him. So he threw a stone and the dog turned his head. That was sense. And while the dog turned his head the boy decided the only way was to stand and fight. That was courage. He strangled the dog. That was victory. See?

CHARLES

Didn't the dog bite him?

JOAN

(*As if to a stupid child*)

You're like the old people in the village—you really believe in miracles. Of course the dog bit him. But I told you the boy had sense, and sense saved his life. God gave man an inside to his head, and He naturally doesn't want to see it wasted. (*Smiles*) See? That's my secret. The witches' secret. What will you pay me for it now?

CHARLES

What do you want?

77

JOAN

The army of France. Believe in God and give me the army.

CHARLES

(*Moves away from her*)
Tomorrow. I'll have time to get ready—

JOAN

(*Moves after him*)
No, right now. You are ready. Come on, Charlie.

CHARLES

Perhaps I am. Perhaps I've been waiting for you and didn't know—(*Laughs nervously*) Shall we send for the Archbishop and La Tremouille and tell them that I have decided to give the army to you? It would be fun to see their faces.

JOAN

Call them.

CHARLES

(*In a panic*)
No. I am frightened.

JOAN

Are you as afraid as you ever can be, ever were or will be, then, now and in the future? Are you sick?

CHARLES

(*Holding his stomach*)

I think so.

JOAN

Good. Good. Then the worst is over. By the time they get scared, you'll be all over yours. Now, if you're as sick as you can get, I'll call them. (*She runs upstage and calls out*) Monseigneur the Archbishop. Monseigneur de la Tremouille. Please come to the Dauphin.

CHARLES

(*Almost happy*)

I am very sick.

JOAN

(*Moves him gently to the throne and arranges his hands and feet*)

God is smiling. He is saying to Himself, "Look at that little Charles. He is sicker than he's ever been in his life.

79

But he has called in his enemies and will face them. My, such a thing is wonderful." (*With great force*) Hang on, Charles. We'll be in Orléans. We'll march right up.

(*The* ARCHBISHOP *and* LA TREMOUILLE *enter, followed by* YOLANDE *and the* COURTIERS.)

ARCHBISHOP

You sent for us, Your Highness?

CHARLES

(*Very sharply*)

I have made a decision. The Royal Army is now under the command of Joan the Virgin Maid, here present. (*Roars out*) I wish to hear no word from you. None.

(*They stare at* CHARLES.)

JOAN

(*Clapping her hands*)

Good. Good, my Charles. You see how simple it is? You're getting better looking, Charles. (CHARLES *giggles. Then he suddenly stops the giggle and stares at* JOAN. *She stares at him. She drops to her knees*) Oh, my God, I thank you.

CHARLES

There is no time to lose. We will need your blessing, sire. Give it to us. (*To* LA TREMOUILLE) Kneel down, sire.

(LA TREMOUILLE, YOLANDE *and the* COURTIERS *drop to their knees. As the* ARCHBISHOP *pronounces the blessing, we hear the chorus sing the* Benedictus. *A* COURT PAGE *gives a sword to* THE DAUPHIN. THE DAUPHIN *gives the sword to* JOAN. WARWICK *comes into the scene and moves downstage to address the audience.*)

WARWICK

In real life, it didn't work out exactly that way. As before, now, and forever, there were long discussions in the French fashion. The council met. Desperate, frightened, with nothing to lose, they decided to dress the girl in battle flags and let her go forth as a symbol of something or other. It worked well. A simple girl inspired simple people to get themselves killed for simple ideals.

(JOAN *rises and moves away from* THE DAUPHIN. *She puts her hand on the sword, and lowers her head in prayer.*)

Curtain

ACT TWO

ACT TWO

Before the curtain rises we hear the music of a soldier's song. The SOLDIERS *sing of* JOAN *and her victories. As the curtain rises we see* JOAN, *in full armor, move across the stage to the music. She carries her sword high above her head in a kind of hero's salute to a group of admiring* VILLAGE WOMEN. *She marches off as* CAUCHON, THE IN-QUISITOR, *and the* JUDGES *take their places.* WARWICK *moves down to address the audience.*

WARWICK

She was in the field. From that day laws of strategy no longer made any difference. We began to lose. They say that Joan worked no miracles at Orléans. They say that our plan of isolated fortresses was absurd, that they could have been taken by anyone who had courage enough to attack. But that is not true. Sir John Talbot was not a fool. He's a good soldier, as he proved long before that miserable business, and after it. By all military laws his fortified positions could not have been broken. And

85

they could not have been broken except by— Well, by what? What shall we call it even now? The unknown, the unguessed—God, if that's the way you believe. The girl was a lark in the skies of France, high over the heads of her soldiers, singing a joyous, crazy song of courage. There she was, outlined against the sun, a target for everybody to shoot at, flying straight and happy into battle. To Frenchmen, she was the soul of France. She was to me, too. (*Smiles, to* CAUCHON) Monseigneur, I like France. Of course, you have your fair share of fools and blackguards. (*Somebody coughs nervously.* WAR-WICK *laughs*) But every once in a while a lark does appear in your sky and then everything stupid and evil is wiped out by the shadow of the lark. I like France very much.

CAUCHON

Your guns prove your affection.

WARWICK

They prove nothing. I love animals but I hunt with guns. (*Sharply*) Too difficult to explain to a man of your simple piety, Monseigneur. So let's get on with the trial. The lark has been captured. The King she crowned, the royal court she saved—for a minute, at least—are about to abandon their little girl. Their loyalty lasted through victory. When we took her prisoner, their luck ran out. They are returning as fast as they can to the old, stale political games.

(CHARLES *and the* ARCHBISHOP *appear.*)

JOAN

(*As she goes back to the trial*)
Charles. (*No answer*) Charles.

CHARLES

(*He turns toward her, then turns away again. He speaks to the* ARCHBISHOP)
I didn't want to send the letter. I tell you I have a feeling that—

ARCHBISHOP

The letter was necessary, sire. We must be rid of the girl now. She is dangerous to us.

CHARLES

I didn't like the letter—

CAUCHON

(*Gently, to* JOAN)

Yesterday Charles disavowed you in a letter sent to all his cities.

JOAN

Charles. (*No answer. To* CAUCHON) Well. He is still my King. And he is your King.

CAUCHON

No, he is not my King. We are loyal subjects of Henry of Lancaster, King of England, King of France. Joan, we love France as much as you do, but we believe that English Henry will put an end to this terrible war. That is why we have taken him as king. The man you call king is, for us, a rebel, claiming a throne that does not belong to him, refusing a good peace because it does not suit his ambitions. He is a puppet man, and we do not wish him as master. (*Sharply*) But I only confuse you. This is not a political trial in which you state your beliefs and we state ours. We are here only to return a lost girl to the bosom of the Sainted Mother Church.

JOAN

(*Pointing to* CHARLES)

That puppet man is the king God gave you. He is a poor, skinny, miserable thing, but given a little time—

CHARLES

(*To the* ARCHBISHOP)

I object as much to being defended in this fashion as I do to being attacked.

ARCHBISHOP

(*Maliciously*)

Let them speak, sire. Turn away. It will be over soon. They will speed up the trial now. They will burn her at the stake.

CHARLES

(*Softly, as if he were sick*)

I hate violence. It makes me sick—

ARCHBISHOP

(*Sharply*)

Count yourself a lucky man. If the English do not condemn her to death, we will have to do it.

CHARLES

I will never do that, Monseigneur. After all, the girl loved me. I will never do that.

ARCHBISHOP

No, sire, certainly not. We will do it for you.
(*They move off.*)

CAUCHON

(*To* JOAN)

You are not stupid, Joan. You can understand what we think. You swear that you heard voices and you swear to the messages they sent you. But because we believe in another king, we cannot believe that it was God Who sent you to fight against us. We are priests but we are men. And man can not believe that God has turned against him.

JOAN

You'll have to believe it when we've beaten you.

CAUCHON

Ah, you answer like a foolish child.

JOAN

My Voices told me—

CAUCHON

How often have we heard those words? Do you think you are the only girl who has ever heard voices?

JOAN

No, I don't think that.

CAUCHON

Not the first and not the last. Every village priest has had his share of young girls in crisis. If the Church believed every sick child—(*Wearily*) You have good sense. You were commander in chief of the army.

JOAN

(*With pride and sudden energy*)
I commanded brave men. *They* believed in me, and *they* followed me.

CAUCHON

Yes. And if on the morning of an attack one of your brave men had suddenly heard Voices that ordered him *not* to follow you, what would you have done with him?

THE LARK

(JOAN *laughs and there is sudden, loud laughter from offstage* SOLDIERS.)

JOAN

(*Calls out toward the laughter*)

The Seigneur Bishop is a priest. He has never been close to you, my soldiers. (*The laughter dies off. Amused, she turns back to* CAUCHON) A good army fights, drinks, rapes—but they don't hear voices.

CAUCHON

A jest is not an answer. You know that a disobedient soldier in your army, in any army in this world, would be silenced. The Church Militant is also an army of this earth and we, its priests, do not believe in the Divine origin of *your* disobedience. Nobody believes in you now, Joan.

JOAN

The common people believe in me—

CAUCHON

They believe in anything. They will follow another leader tomorrow. You are alone, all alone.

92

JOAN

I think as I think. You have the right to punish me for it.

CAUCHON

You are strong and you are stubborn, but that is not a sign that God is on your side.

JOAN

When something is black I cannot say that it is white.

THE PROMOTER

(*Rises and speaks angrily to* JOAN)
What spell did you cast upon the man you call your King? By what means did you force him to give his armies to you?

JOAN

I have told you. I cast no spell upon him.

THE PROMOTER

It is said that you gave him a piece of mandrake.

JOAN

I don't know what mandrake is.

93

THE LARK

THE PROMOTER

Your secret has a name. We want to know what it is.

JOAN

(*Sharply*)

I gave him courage. That is the only word I know for
what was between us. When a girl says one word of good
sense and people listen to her, that's proof that God is
present and no strange spells or miracles are needed.

LADVENU

(*Softly*)

Now there is a good and humble answer, Monseigneur.
An answer that cannot be held against her.

THE PROMOTER

I do not agree. She is saying that she does not believe
in the miracles as they are taught in our Holy Book. (*To*
JOAN) You declare that you deny the act of Jesus at the
Marriage of Cana? You declare that you deny the miracle raising of Lazarus from the dead?

JOAN

No, Messire. Our Seigneur changed the water into
wine and retied the thread of Lazarus' life. But for Him

Who is Master of life and death, that is no more miracle than if I were to make thread for my loom.

THE PROMOTER

(*With great anger, to the* JUDGES)
Mark her words. Write them down. She says that Jesus made no miracles.

JOAN

(*Runs toward the* JUDGES *with great force*)
I say that true miracles are not tricks performed by gypsies in a village square. True miracles are created by men when they use the courage and intelligence that God gave them.

CAUCHON

You are saying to us, *to us,* that the real miracle of God on this earth is man. Man, who is naught but sin and error, impotent against his own wickedness—

JOAN

And man is also strength and courage and splendor in his most desperate minutes. I know man because I have seen him. He is a miracle.

LADVENU

(*Quickly, nervously*)

Monseigneur, Joan speaks an awkward language. But she speaks from the heart, and without guile. Perhaps when we press down upon her, we risk making her say here what she does not mean.

THE PROMOTER

(*To* JOAN)

Do you believe that man is the greatest miracle of God?

JOAN

Yes, Messire.

THE PROMOTER

(*Shouts*)

You blaspheme. Man is impurity and lust. The dark acts of his nights are the acts of a beast—

JOAN

Yes, Messire. And the same man who acts the beast will rise from a brothel bed and throw himself before a blade to save the soldier who walks beside him. Nobody knows why he does. He doesn't know. But he does it, and he dies, cleansed and shining. He has done both good and evil, and thus twice acted like a man. That makes God happy because God made him for just this contradiction. We are good and we are evil, and that is what was meant.

> (*There is indignant movement among the* JUDGES. THE INQUISITOR *rises, holds up his hand. Immediately there is silence. They have been waiting for him to speak.*)

THE INQUISITOR

I have at no time spoken. (*To* JOAN) I speak to you now. I represent here the Holy Inquisition of which I am the Vicar for France. I have arrived from the south of Spain, and have little knowledge of the French and English war. It does not concern me whether Charles or the Lancaster Henry rules over France. It does not concern me that the French Duke of Burgundy has joined the English, and thus Frenchman fights French brother. They are all children of the Church. Nor have I interest in defending the temporal integrity of the Church in these quarrels. (*Turns toward* CAUCHON) We leave such matters to our bishops and our priests. (*Bows to* CAUCHON) Nor time to be curious about the kindness and humanity which seem to move the judgment. (*Sharply, toward* THE PROMOTER) Nor do we find interest in these endless dreams of the Devil that haunt the nights of the Promoter. The Holy Inquisition fights in the dark world of night, against an enemy it alone can recognize. (*Stops, moves toward* WARWICK) We do not care that the princes of the earth have sometimes laughed at the vigilance with which we hunt the enemy, the time and thought that we give to the judgment of the enemy. The princes of the earth are sometimes hurrying and shallow men. They remove their enemies with a length of rope and, in the crudeness of their thinking, they believe the danger ended there. We hear the mocking laughter of such men and we forgive it. The Holy Inquisition concerns itself in matters unknown to temporal kings. Our enemy is a great enemy and has a great name. (*To* JOAN) You know his name?

JOAN

No, Messire. I do not understand you.

THE INQUISITOR

You will understand me. Stand up. You will answer now to me. Are you a Christian?

THE LARK

Yes, Messire.

The trees that shaded the village church threw shad-
ows on the house of your father. The bells of the church
brought you to prayer and sent you to work. The men we
sent to your village all bring the same word: you were a
pious girl.

Yes, Messire.

You were a tender little girl. And you were a tender
woman. You cried for the wounded in every battle—

Yes. I cried for the wounded. They were French.

And you cried for the English. You stayed with a
wounded English soldier who screamed through a night
of pain. You held him until he died, calling him your
child and giving him a hope of Heaven.

JOAN

You know that, Messire?

THE INQUISITOR

Yes. The Holy Inquisition knows much of you, Joan. Grave considerate talk was given to you. And they sent me here to judge you.

LADVENU

Messire Inquisitor, Joan has always acted with kindness and Christian charity, but this court has buried it in silence. I am happy to hear you remind them that—

THE INQUISITOR

(*Sternly*)

Silence, Brother Ladvenu. I ask you not to forget that the Holy Inquisition alone is qualified to distinguish between theological virtues and that troubled brew that man so boastfully calls the milk of human kindness. (*Turns to the* JUDGES) Ah, my masters. What strange matters concern you all. Your business is to defend the Faith. But you see the kind eyes of a young girl and you are overwhelmed.

LADVENU

Our Lord loved with charity and kindness, Messire. He said to a sinner, "Go in peace." He said—

THE INQUISITOR

Silence, I said to you, Brother Ladvenu. (*Softly, carefully*) You are young. I am told your learning is very great and that is why you were admitted to this trial. Therefore I am hopeful that experience will teach you not to translate the great words into the vulgar tongue, nor embroider the meaning to suit your heart. Be seated and be silent. (*He turns back to* JOAN) You were very young when you first heard your Voices.

JOAN

Yes, Messire.

THE INQUISITOR

I am going to shock you: there is nothing very exceptional about the Voices you heard in those days. Our archives are full of such cases. There are many young visionaries. Girls frequently experience a crisis of mysticism. It passes. But with you—and your priest should have recognized it—the crisis was prolonged. The messages became precise and the Celestial Voices began to use most unusual words.

JOAN

Yes. My Voices told me to go and save the Kingdom of France.

THE INQUISITOR

A strange order to an ignorant peasant girl.

JOAN

Not so strange, Messire, because it turned out to be the truth.

THE INQUISITOR

I say a strange order to a girl who had seen nothing of war. The troubles of France could have been no more to you than tales told at twilight. And yet suddenly you went out into the great world of kings and battles, convinced that it was your mission to aid your brothers in their struggle to keep the land on which they were born, and which they imagine belongs to them.

JOAN

Our Lord could not want the English to kill us and to conquer us. He could not want us to live by their laws and wishes. When they have gone back across the sea, to their own land, I will not go and pick a quarrel with them. They can rest easy in their own house. I've always said that.

THE INQUISITOR

(*Sternly*)

And I say your presumption is not suited to my taste.

LADVENU

She did not mean, Messire—she speaks in a youthful fashion.

CAUCHON

(*Softly*)

Be still, Brother Ladvenu.

THE INQUISITOR

(*To* JOAN)

It would have been more fitting for a pious girl to have spent her life in prayers and penitence and, in such manner, obtained from Heaven the promise that the English would be defeated.

JOAN

I did all that. But I think you must first strike and then pray. That's the way God wants it. I had to explain to Charles how to attack. And he believed me and Dunois believed me and La Hire—good men, wild bulls they were, and warriors. Ah, we had some fine battles together. It was good, in the dawn, riding boot to boot with friends—

THE PROMOTER

To the kill. Did your Voices instruct you to kill?

JOAN

(*Angrily*)

I have never killed a man. But war is war.

CAUCHON

You love war, Joan.

JOAN

(*Softly*)

Yes. And that is one of the sins from which God will have to absolve me. But I did not like pain or death. At night, on the battlefield, I would weep for the dead—

THE LARK

THE PROMOTER

You would weep at night for the dead but by morning
you were shouting for a new battle.

JOAN

(Moves to him, with great force)

I say God did not wish one Englishman to remain in
France. That's not so hard to understand, is it? We had to
do our work, that's all. You are wise men, you think too
much. Your heads are filled with too much celestial sci-
ence. You don't understand even the simplest things any
more—things that my dullest soldier would understand
without talk. Isn't that true, La Hire?

*(She stumbles, moves away from the JUDGES, and
falls to the ground. The lights dim on the trial and
we hear again the whistling of the soldier's song.
LA HIRE, in full armor, appears upstage and moves
toward JOAN.)*

LA HIRE

The morning has come, Madame Joan.

(She sits up, shivers, stares at LA HIRE.)

JOAN

The night was cold, La Hire. (*He sits beside her, warms her hands in his own.* JOAN *looks toward the trial, then up, then back to* LA HIRE, *as if she were confused by the place and the time*) Good La Hire. Great La Hire. You've really come to help me as I knew you would.

LA HIRE

(*He takes out an onion and begins to peel it*)
Come to help you? I was sleeping fifty feet from you, Madame Joan, watching over you as I always do. (*She laughs and moves closer to him*) Don't come too close. I stink of wine and onions.

JOAN

No, no. You smell fine.

LA HIRE

Usually you tell me I stink too much to be a Christian. You say I am a danger to the army because if the wind is behind me the English will know where we are.

JOAN

Oh, La Hire, I was so stupid in those days. You know how girls are. Nothing ever happens to them, they know nothing, but they pretend they know everything. But I am not so stupid any more. You smell good because you smell like a man.

LA HIRE

I can't stand a man who washes in the field because to me a man like that isn't a man. I was brought up on an onion in the morning. The rest can have their sausage. The smell is more distinguished, you tell me. I know you think a breakfast onion is a sin.

JOAN

(Laughs)

A breakfast onion is not a sin. Nothing that is true is a sin, La Hire. I was a fool. I tormented you. But I didn't know anything then. I didn't. *(Softly)* Ah, you smell so good. Sweat, onions, wine. You have all the smells a man should have. And you curse, you kill, and you think of nothing but women.

LA HIRE

Me?

JOAN

You. But I tell you that with all your sins you are like a bright new coin in the hand of God.

LA HIRE

Well, I have had a bastard life and when I go into battle, I say my prayers. I say, "God, I hope You'll help me as I would help You if You faced those God damned"—

JOAN

(*Shocked*)

La Hire!

LA HIRE

(*Softly*)

To tell you the truth, I'm frightened of what will happen to me if I get killed.

JOAN

Paradise will happen to you. They are looking forward to having you with them.

LA HIRE

That gives me heart, Madame Joan. I've always wanted to go to Paradise. But if it's all full of saints and bishops, I might not be too happy—

JOAN

It's full of men like you. It's the others who are kept waiting at the gates—(*Suddenly*) The gates. The gates of

Orléans. They're ahead of us—the day has come, La
Hire. To horse, my boy, to horse. (*She climbs on her stool.*
LA HIRE *stands next to her. They hold imaginary reins in
their hands as they ride imaginary horses*) It's dawn, La
Hire. The woods are still wet from the night, the trees
are still dark and strange. It's fine to ride into battle with
a good soldier by your side.

LA HIRE

Some people don't like it. Some people like to make a
little garden out of life and walk down a path.

JOAN

But they never know what we know. (*As if she were
puzzled and ashamed*) Death has to be waiting at the end
of the ride before you truly see the earth, and feel your
heart, and love the world. (*Suddenly, in a whisper*) There
are three English soldiers. (*She looks back*) We've out-
ridden the others. We are alone.

LA HIRE

Get off your horse, Madame Joan. Lead him back. You
have never used your sword.

JOAN

No. Don't meet them alone, La Hire—

LA HIRE

(*He draws his sword*)

I'll kill them . . . God damned English bastards.

(*Sword in hand, he disappears.*)

JOAN

(*Kneels in prayer*)

Dear God, he is as good as bread. I answer for him. He's my friend. (*She turns toward the* JUDGES, *angry, defiant*) The last word will not be spoken at this trial. La Hire will come to deliver me. He will bring three hundred lancers, I know them all, and they will take me from my prison—

CAUCHON

Yes. They came to deliver you, Joan.

JOAN

(*Running to him*)

Where are they? I knew they would come—

CAUCHON

They came to the gates of the city. When they saw how many English soldiers were here, they turned and went away.

110

JOAN

(*Shaken*)

Ah. They turned and went away. Without fighting? (CAUCHON *turns away*) Yes. Of course. It was *I* who taught them to do just that. I would say to them, "Have a little sense. It doesn't cost a sou. Learn not to be brave when you are outnumbered, unless—(*Violently*) That's what they did. They went to get reinforcements for me—

CAUCHON

No. Your friends will not return, Joan.

JOAN

That's not true. "Learn not to be brave when you are outnumbered," I said, "*unless* you can't retreat. Then you must fight because there is no other way—" (*Proudly*) La Hire will return. Because there is no other way to save me now.

CAUCHON

La Hire sells himself to whichever prince has need. When he discovered that your Charles was tired of war and would sign any peace, he marched his men toward Germany. He looks for a new land on which to try his sword. (*Comes to her*) You have been abandoned. It will

111

sound strange to you, but the priests of this court are the only men who care for your soul and for your life. Humble yourself, Joan, and the Church will take your hand. In your heart, you are a child of the Church.

JOAN

(*Softly*)

Yes.

CAUCHON

Trust yourself to the Church. She will weigh your deeds and take from you the agony of self-judgment.

JOAN

(*After a long silence*)

For that which is of the Faith, I turn to the Church, as I have always done. But what I am, I will not denounce. What I have done, I will not deny.

> (*There is a shocked silence. Then there is great movement in the courtroom, as if this were the answer that would bring the judgment.* THE INQUISITOR *rises. The* PRIESTS *are suddenly silent.* THE INQUISITOR *slowly moves before the* PRIESTS, *peering into their faces. The* PRIESTS *draw back, frightened.*)

THE INQUISITOR

(*To one* PRIEST)

Not you. (*To another* PRIEST) Not you. (*To a third*
PRIEST) Not you. (*Pauses before* CAUCHON, *stares at him*)
And not you, Bishop of Beauvais. I have spoken of the
great enemy, but not even now do you know his name.
You do not understand on whom you sit in judgment,
nor the issues of the judgment. I have told you that the
Holy Inquisition is not concerned with royal rank or
merchant gold or peasant birth. To us, a scholar in his
room is equal in importance to an emperor in his palace.
Because *we* know the name of our enemy. His name is
natural man. (*There is silence.* LADVENU *moves forward*)
Can you not see that this girl is the symbol of that which
is most to be feared? She is the enemy. She is man as he
stands against us. Look at her. Frightened, hungry,
dirty, abandoned by all, and no longer even sure that
those Voices in the air ever spoke to her at all. Does her
misery make her a suppliant begging God for mercy and
for light? No. She turns away from God. She dares to
stand under torture, thrashing about like a proud beast
in the stable of her dungeon. She raises her eyes, not to
God, but to man's image of himself. I have need to remind you, Masters, that he who loves Man does not
love God.

LADVENU

(*With great force*)

It cannot be. Jesus Himself became a man.

THE INQUISITOR

(*Turns to* CAUCHON)

Seigneur Bishop, I must ask you to send your young assessor from this courtroom. I will consider after this session whether he may return or whether I will bring charges against him. (*Shouts*) Against him, or against any other. *Any* other. I would bring charges against myself if God should let me lose my way.

CAUCHON

(*Softly*)

Leave us, Brother Ladvenu.

LADVENU

Messire Inquisitor, I owe you obedience. I will not speak again. But I will pray to our Lord Jesus that you remember the weakness of your small, sad, lonely—enemy.

(LADVENU *exits.*)

THE INQUISITOR

Do you have need to question her further? To ask all the heavy words that are listed in your legal papers?

What need to ask her why she still persists in wearing man's dress when it is contrary to the commandments? Why she dared the sin of living among men as a man? The deeds no longer matter. What she has done is of less importance than why she did it, the answers less important than the one answer. It is a fearful answer, "What I am, I will not . . ." You wish to say it again? Say it.

JOAN
(*Slowly, softly*)

What I am, I will not denounce. What I have done, I will not deny.

THE INQUISITOR
(*Carefully, as if he has taken the measure of an enemy*)

You have heard it. Down through the ages, from dungeon, from torture chamber, from the fire of the stake. Ask her and she will say with those others, "Take my life. I will give it because I will not deny what I have done." This is what they say, all of them, the insolent breed. The men who dare our God. Those who say no to us—(*He moves toward* JOAN. CAUCHON *rises*) Well, you and all like you shall be made to say yes. You put the Idea in peril, and that you will not be allowed to do. (*Turns to the* JUDGES) The girl is only a monstrous symbol of the faith decayed. Therefore I now demand her immediate punishment. I demand that she be excommunicated from the Church. I demand that she be returned to secular authority there to receive her punishment. I ask the secular arm to limit her sentence to this side of death and the mutilation of her members.

(CAUCHON *moves to* THE INQUISITOR *as if to stop the judgment.*)

WARWICK
(*To* CAUCHON)

A passionate man and so sincere. I think he means simply to throw the dirty work to me. I am the secular authority here. Why didn't your French Charles have her burned? It was his job.

CHARLES
(*Very disturbed*)

I don't want to do it. I don't like killing.
(*A large, masked figure appears.*)

CAUCHON
(*Calls to the masked man*)

Master Executioner, is the wood for the stake dry and ready to burn?

EXECUTIONER

All is ready. Things will go according to custom. But I will not be able to help the girl this time.

CAUCHON

What do you mean help her, Master?

EXECUTIONER

We let the first flames rise high. Then I climb up behind the victims and strangle them the rest of the way. It's easier and quicker for everybody. But I have had special instructions this time to make the fire very high. And so it will take longer and I will not be able to reach her for the act of mercy.

CAUCHON

(*Moves to* JOAN)

Did you hear that?

JOAN

I've remembered a dream from years ago. I woke screaming and ran to my mother—(*Screams as if in pain*) Ah.

CAUCHON

(*Desperately*)

Joan, for the last time I offer you the saving hand of your Mother Church. We wish to save you, but we can delay no longer. The crowd has been waiting since dawn. They eat their food, scold their children, make jokes, and grow impatient. You are famous and they have nothing better to do with their lives than bring garlands to the famous—or watch them burn.

JOAN

(*As if she is still in the dream*)

I forgive them, Messire. I forgive you, too.

THE PROMOTER

(*Furiously*)

Monseigneur speaks to you like a father in order to save your miserable soul and you answer by forgiving him.

JOAN

Monseigneur speaks to me gently, he takes great pains to seduce me, but I do not know whether he means to save me or conquer me. In any case, he will be obliged to have me burned.

CAUCHON
(*Comes to her*)

For the last time I say: Confess your sins and return to us. We will save you.

JOAN
(*She clings to his robe*)

I wish to return to the Church. I want the Holy Communion. I have asked for it over and over again. But they have refused to give it to me.

CAUCHON

After your confession, when you have begun your penance, we will give it to you. (*There is no answer. Very softly*) Are you not afraid to die?

JOAN

Yes. I am afraid. What difference does that make? I've always been so afraid of fire. (*Gasps*) I've remembered a dream—

CAUCHON
(*Pulls her to him*)

Joan, we cannot believe in the Divinity of your Voices. But if we are wrong—and certainly that thought has crossed our minds—

119

THE LARK

THE PROMOTER

(*Furious*)

No, I say no. Even to you, my Bishop of Beauvais—

CAUCHON

(*To* JOAN)

But if we are wrong then we will have committed a monstrous sin of ignorance and we will pay for it the rest of our eternal lives. But we are the priests of your Church. Trust our belief that we are right, as you trusted your good village priest. Place yourself in our hands. You will be at peace.

JOAN

I cannot follow what you say. I am tired. Oh, sire, I do not sleep at night. I come here and all is said so fast that I cannot understand. You torture me with such gentle words, and your voice is so kind. I would rather have you beat me—

CAUCHON

I talk to you thus because my pride is less than yours.

JOAN

(*She moves away from him, as if she were sick and wanted to be alone*)

Pride? I have been a prisoner so long—I think my head is sick and old, and the bottom of me does not hold any

120

more. Sometimes I don't know where I am and my dungeon seems a great beech tree. I am hungry, or I was, and I want a taste of country milk—

CAUCHON

(Desperately, as if he were at the end)

Look at me, Joan, keep your mind here. I am an old man. I have killed people in the defense of my beliefs. I am so close to death myself that I do not wish to kill again. I do not wish to kill a little girl. Be kind. (*Cries out*) Help me to save you.

JOAN

(Very softly; broken now)

What do you want me to say? Please tell me in simple words.

CAUCHON

I am going to ask you three questions. Answer yes three times. That is all. (*With passion*) Help me, Joan.

JOAN

But could I sleep a few hours, sire?

CAUCHON

No! We cannot wait. Do you entrust yourself with humility to the Holy Roman and Apostolic Church, to our Holy Father, the Pope, and to his bishops? Will you rely upon them, and upon no one else, to be your judges? Do you make the complete and total act of submission? Do you ask to be returned to the bosom of the Church?

JOAN

Yes, but—(THE INQUISITOR *rises*. CAUCHON *becomes nervous*) I don't want to say the opposite of what my Voices told me. I don't ever want to bear false witness against Charlie. I fought so hard for the glory of his consecration. Oh, that was a day when he was crowned. The sun was out—

CHARLES

(*To* JOAN)

It was a nice day and I'll always remember it. But I'd rather not think it was a divine miracle. I'd rather people didn't think that God sent you to me. Because now that you're a prisoner, and thought to be a heretic and a sorceress, they think that God has abandoned me. I'm in bad enough trouble without that kind of gossip. Just forget about me and go your way.

(JOAN *bows her head.*)

CAUCHON

Do you wish me to repeat the question? (JOAN *does not answer.* CAUCHON *is angry*) Are you mad? You understand now that we are your only protectors, that this is the last thing I can do for you? You cannot bargain and quibble like a peasant at a village fair. You are an impudent girl, and I now become angry with you. You should be on your knees to the Church.

JOAN

(*Falls to her knees*)

Messire, deep in your heart do you believe that our Lord wishes me to submit to the judgment?

CAUCHON

I so believe.

JOAN

(*Softly*)

Then I submit.

(*There is great movement in the court.* THE INQUISITOR *rises;* THE PROMOTER *moves to him.*)

CAUCHON

(*Very tired now*)

You promise to renounce forever the bearing of arms?

JOAN

But, Messire, there is still so much to do—

CAUCHON

(*Angrily*)

Nothing more will ever be done by you.

WARWICK

That is true, Joan.

CHARLES

And if you're thinking of helping me again, please don't. I won't ever use you any more. It would be very dangerous for me.

JOAN

(*Broken now, almost as if she were asleep*)

I renounce forever the bearing of arms.

CAUCHON

(*In great haste*)

Do you renounce forever the wearing of that brazen uniform?

THE LARK

JOAN

You have asked me that over and over again. The uniform doesn't matter. My Voices told me to put it on.

THE PROMOTER

It was the Devil who told you to put it on.

JOAN

Oh, Messire, put away the Devil for today. My Voices chose the uniform because my Voices have good sense. (*With great effort*) I had to ride with soldiers. It was necessary they not think of me as a girl. It was necessary they see in me nothing but a soldier like themselves. That is all the sense there was to it.

CAUCHON

But why have you persisted in wearing it in prison? You have been asked this question in many examinations and your refusal to answer has become of great significance to your judges.

JOAN

And I have asked over and over to be taken to a Church prison. Then I would take off my man's uniform.

THE LARK

THE PROMOTER

(*To* CAUCHON)

Monseigneur, the girl is playing with us, as from the first. I do not understand what she says or why you—

JOAN

(*Angry*)

One doesn't have to be an educated man to understand what I am saying.

THE PROMOTER

(*Turns to* JUDGES)

She says that she submits to the Church. But I tell you that as long as she refuses to put aside that Devil dress, I will exercise my rights as master judge of heretics and witchcraft. (*To* CAUCHON) Strange pressures have been put upon all of us. I know not from where they come, but I tell even you—

JOAN

I have said that if you put me in a Church prison I will take off this uniform.

THE PROMOTER

You will not bargain. Put aside that dress or, no matter who feels otherwise, you will be declared a sorceress.

JOAN
(Softly, to CAUCHON)

I am not alone in prison. Two English soldier guards are in the cell with me night and day. The nights are long. I am in chains. I try hard not to sleep, but sometimes I am too tired—(*She stops, embarrassed*) In this uniform it is easier for me to defend myself.

CAUCHON
(In great anger)

Have you had so to defend yourself since the beginning of this trial?

(WARWICK *moves to* JOAN.)

JOAN

Every night since I've been captured. I don't have much sleep. In the mornings, when I am brought before you, I am confused, and I don't understand your questions. I told you that. Sometimes I try to sleep here in the trial so that I will stay awake in the night—

CAUCHON

Why haven't you told us this before?

JOAN

Because the soldiers told me they would be hanged if I said anything—

WARWICK

(*Very angry*)

They were right. (*To* CAUCHON) Detestable bastards. It's disgusting. They've learned such things since they came to France. It may be all right in the French Army, but not in mine. (*Bows to* JOAN) I am sorry, Madame. It will not happen again.

CAUCHON

(*To* JOAN)

The Church will protect you from now on. I promise you.

JOAN

Then I agree to put on woman's dress.

CAUCHON

Thank you, my child. That is all. (*He moves to* THE INQUISITOR) Messire Inquisitor, Brother Ladvenu drew up the Act of Renunciation. Will you permit me to recall him here? (*With bitterness*) The girl has said yes, this man has said yes.

THE PROMOTER

(*To* THE INQUISITOR)

Messire Inquisitor, you are going to allow this to happen?

THE LARK

THE INQUISITOR

If she said yes, she has fulfilled the only condition that concerns me.

THE PROMOTER

(*Turns to* CAUCHON)

This trial has been conducted with an indulgence that is beyond my understanding. (*To* THE INQUISITOR) I am told that there are those here who eat from the English manger. I ask myself now if they have arranged to eat better from the French manger.

THE INQUISITOR

(*Rises, moves toward* JOAN)

It is not a question of mangers, Messire Promoter. *I* ask myself how did it happen that this girl said yes when so many lesser ones did not bow the head. I had not believed it to be possible. (*Points to* CAUCHON) And why was tenderness born in the heart of that old man who was her judge? He is at the end of a life worn out with compromise and debasement. Why now, here, for this girl, this dangerous girl, did his heart—(*He kneels, ignoring the others. As he prays, we hear only the words . . .*) Why, Oh Lord . . . ? Why, Oh Lord . . . ? Consecrate it in peace to Your Glory. . . . Your Glory—

THE LARK

CAUCHON

(*As* LADVENU *enters*)

Please read the act.

LADVENU

(*Comes to* JOAN. *With great tenderness*)

I have prayed for you, Joan. (*Reading*) "I, Joan, commonly called The Maid, confess having sinned through pride and malice in pretending to have received revelations from our Lord God. I confess I have blasphemed by wearing an immodest costume. I have incited men to kill through witchcraft and I here confess to it. I swear on the Holy Gospels I will not again wear this heretic's dress and I swear never to bear arms again. I declare that I place myself humbly at the mercy of our Holy Mother Church and our Holy Father, the Pope of Rome and His Bishops, so that they may judge my sins and my errors. I beseech Her to receive me in Her Bosom and I declare myself ready to submit to the sentence which She may inflict upon me. In faith of which, I have signed my name upon this Act of Renunciation of which I have full knowledge. (LADVENU *hands the pen to* JOAN. *She moves it in the air, as if she had not heard and did not understand.* LADVENU *takes her hand and puts it on the paper*) I will help you.

CAUCHON

(As if he were a very old man)

You have been saved. We, your judges, in mercy and mitigation, now condemn you to spend the remainder of your days in prison. There you will do penance for your sins. You will eat the bread of sorrow and drink the water of anguish until, through solitary contemplation, you repent. Under these conditions of penance, we declare you delivered of the danger of excommunication. You may go in peace. (*He makes the Sign of the Cross*) Take her away.

> (CAUCHON *stumbles and is helped by* LADVENU. *A* SOLDIER *pushes* JOAN *away from the trial. The* JUDGES *rise and slowly move off.* CAUCHON *moves past* WARWICK.)

WARWICK

There were several times, sire, when I thought I would have to interfere. My King must have what he paid for. But you were right and I was wrong. The making of a martyr is dangerous business. The pile of faggots, the invincible girl in the flames, might have been a triumph for the French spirit. But the apologies of a hero are sad and degrading. You did well, sire; you are a wise man.

131

CAUCHON

(*With great bitterness*)

I did not mean to earn your praise.

(*He moves off. The lights dim on the trial as* WAR-WICK *moves off. Four* SOLDIERS *appear with spears, and their spears become the bars of* JOAN's *jail cell.* CHARLES *appears and stands looking at* JOAN *through the bars.*)

CHARLES

I didn't want you to sacrifice yourself for me, Joan. I know you loved me, but I don't want people to love me. It makes for obligations. This filthy prison air is wet and stinks. Don't they ever clean these places? (*He peers into her cell, sees the water pail that sits beside her, and draws back*) Tell them to give you fresh water. My God, what goes on in this world. (*She does not answer him*) Don't you want to speak to me, Joan?

JOAN

Good-bye, Charlie.

CHARLES

You must stop calling me Charlie. Ever since my coronation I am careful to make everyone say sire.

JOAN

Sire.

CHARLES

I'll come and see you again. Good-bye.

(*He moves off.* JOAN *lies in silence. Then she tries to drink from the water pail, retches, and puts her hand over her mouth as if she were very sick.*)

JOAN

Blessed Saint Michael. (*She makes a strange sound, shivers*) I am in prison. Come to me. Find me. (*Cries out*) I need you now. (*Very loudly*) I told you that I was afraid of fire, long before I ever knew—or did I always know? You want me to live? (*When there is no answer*) Why do I call for help? You must have good reason for not coming to me. (*She motions toward courtroom*) They think I dreamed it all. Maybe I did. But it's over now . . .

(WARWICK *comes slowly into the cell.*)

WARWICK

(*Hesitantly*)

You are weeping?

JOAN

No, Monseigneur.

WARWICK

I am sorry to disturb you. I only came to say that I am glad you are saved. You behaved damned well. I, er, well, it's rather difficult to say in my language, but the plain fact is that I like you. And it amused me to watch you with the Inquisitor. Sinister man, isn't he? I detest these intellectual idealists more than anything in the world. What disgusting animals they are. He wanted only to see you humiliate yourself, no matter your state or your misery. And when you did, he was satisfied.

JOAN
(Softly)
He had reason to be satisfied.

WARWICK

Well, don't worry about him. It all worked out well. Martyrs are likely to stir the blood of simple people and set up too grand a monument to themselves. It's all very complex and dangerous. Tell me, are you a virgin?

JOAN

Yes.

WARWICK

I knew you were. A woman would not talk as you do. My fiancée in England is a very pure girl and she also talks like a boy. You are the greatest horsewoman I have ever seen. (*When there is no answer*) Ah, well. I am intruding on you. Don't hesitate to let me know if I can ever do anything for you. Good-bye, madame.

JOAN

Nobody else came to see me here. You are a kind man, Monseigneur.

WARWICK

Not at all. (*Motions toward courtroom*) It's that I don't like all those fellows who use words to make war. You and I killed because that was the way things turned out for us.

JOAN

Monseigneur, I have done wrong. And I don't know how or why I did it. (*Slowly, bitterly*) I swore against myself. That is a great sin, past all others—(*Desperately*) I still believe in all that I did, and yet I swore against it. God can't want that. What can be left for me?

135

WARWICK

Certainly they are not going to make you a gay life, not at first. But things work out and in time your nasty little Charles might even show you a speck of loyalty—

JOAN

Yes, when I am no longer dangerous, he might even give me a small pension and a servant's room at court.

WARWICK

(*Sharply*)

Madame, there will be no court.

JOAN

And I will wear cast-off brocade and put jewels in my hair and grow old. I will be happy that few people remember my warrior days and I will grovel before those who speak of my past and pray them to be silent. And when I die, in a big fat bed, I will be remembered as a crazy girl who rode into battle for what she said she believed, and ate the dirt of lies when she was faced with punishment. That will be the best that I can have—if my little Charles remembers me at all. If he doesn't there will be a prison dungeon, and filth and darkness—(*Cries out*) What good is life either way?

136

WARWICK

It is good any way you can have it. We all try to save a
little honor, of course, but the main thing is to be here—

JOAN

(Rises, calls out, speaking to the Voices)
I was only born the day you first spoke to me. My life
only began on the day you told me what I must do, my
sword in hand. You are silent, dear my God, because you
are sad to see me frightened and craven. And for what?
A few years of unworthy life. *(She kneels. Softly, as if she
is answering a message)* I know. Yes, I know. I took the
good days from You and refused the bad. I know. Dear
my God forgive me, and keep me now to be myself. Forgive me and take me back for what I am. *(She rises. She
is happy and cheerful)* Call your soldiers, Warwick. I
deny my confession.

WARWICK

Joan. No nonsense, please. Things are all right as they
are. I—

JOAN

Come.
(She holds out her hand to him.)

137

WARWICK

I don't want anything to do with your death.

JOAN

(Smiles)

You have a funny gentleman's face. But you are kind. Come now. *(She calls out)* Soldiers! Englishmen! Give me back my warrior clothes. And when I have put them on, call back all the priests. *(Stops, puts her hands in prayer and speaks simply)* Please God, help me now.

> *(The music of the "Sanctus" begins as the* JUDGES, CAUCHON, THE INQUISITOR, THE PROMOTER, CHARLES, *the* PEOPLE OF THE COURT, *return to the stage. Two* SOLDIERS *bring a crude stake.* JOAN *herself moves to the stake and the* SOLDIERS *lash her to it. Other* SOLDIERS *and* VILLAGE WOMEN *pick up the bundles of faggots and carry them off stage. The* EXECUTIONER *appears with lighted torch and moves through the crowd.)*

JOAN

(As they are about to carry her off)

Please. Please. Give me a Cross.

THE PROMOTER

No Cross will be given to a witch.

AN ENGLISH SOLDIER

(*He has taken two sticks of wood and made a Cross. Now he hands his Cross to* JOAN)

Here, my daughter. Here's your Cross. (*Very angry, to* THE PROMOTER) She has a right to a Cross like anybody else.

> (JOAN *is carried off stage. The lights dim and we see flames—or the shadows of flames—as they are projected on the cyclorama.* LADVENU *runs on stage with a Cross from the church and stands holding it high for* JOAN *to see.*)

THE INQUISITOR

(*Calling to* EXECUTIONER)

Be quick. Be quick. Let the smoke hide her. (*To* WARWICK) In five minutes, Monseigneur, the world will be crying.

WARWICK

Yes.

THE INQUISITOR

(*Shouting to* EXECUTIONER)

Be quick, master, be quick.

EXECUTIONER

(*Calling in to him*)

All is ready, messire. The flames reach her now.

LADVENU

(*Calling out*)

Courage, Joan. We pray for you.

CAUCHON

May God forgive us all.

(CAUCHON *falls to his knees and begins the prayer for the dead. The prayers are murmured as the chorus chants a Requiem. The* SOLDIERS *and the* VILLAGE PEOPLE *return to the stage: a* WOMAN *falls to the ground; a* SOLDIER *cries out; a* GIRL *bends over as if in pain and a* SOLDIER *helps her to move on; the* COURT LADIES *back away, hiding their faces from the burning; the* PRIESTS *kneel in prayer.*)

THE LARK

CHARLES

(*In a whisper as he leaves*)
What does she do? What does she say? Is it over?

THE INQUISITOR

(*To* LADVENU)
What does she do?

LADVENU

She is quiet.

THE INQUISITOR

(*Moves away*)
Is her head lowered?

LADVENU

No, messire. Her head is high.

THE INQUISITOR

(*As if he were in pain*)
Ah. (*To* LADVENU) She falters now?

LADVENU

No. It is a terrible and noble sight, messire. You should
turn and see.

THE INQUISITOR

(*Moves off*)

I have seen it all before.

(*The lights dim.* CAUCHON *rises from his prayers. He stumbles and falls.* LADVENU *and* WARWICK *move to help him. He takes* LADVENU'S *arm, but moves away from* WARWICK, *refusing his help. As the stage becomes dark,* CAUCHON, THE PRO- MOTER, LADVENU *and* WARWICK *move downstage and the light comes up on* LA HIRE *who stands above them.* LA HIRE *is in full armor, holding helmet and sword.*)

LA HIRE

You were fools to burn Joan of Arc.

CAUCHON

We committed a sin, a monstrous sin.

WARWICK

Yes, it was a grave mistake. We made a lark into a giant bird who will travel the skies of the world long after our names are forgotten, or confused, or cursed down.

THE LARK

LA HIRE

I knew the girl and I loved her. You can't let it end this way. If you do, it will not be the true story of Joan.

LADVENU

That is right. The true story of Joan is not the hideous agony of a girl tied to a burning stake. She will stand forever for the glory that can be. Praise God.

LA HIRE

The true story of Joan is the story of her happiest day. Anybody with any sense knows that. Go back and act it out.

> (*The lights dim on the four men and come up on the Coronation of Charles in Reims Cathedral. The altar cloth is in place, the lighted candles are behind the altar, stained glass windows are projected on the cyclorama. The* ARCHBISHOP *appears, and the people of the royal court.* JOAN *stands clothed in a fine white robe, ornamented with a fleur-de-lis.*)

WARWICK

(*Moves into the coronation scene, stares bewildered as* CHARLES, *in coronation robes, carrying his crown, crosses to the altar*)

This could not have been her happiest day. To watch Holy Oil being poured on that mean, sly little head!

CHARLES

(*Turns to* WARWICK, *amused*)

Oh, I didn't turn out so bad. I drove you out of the country. And I got myself some money before I died. I was as good as most.

WARWICK

So you were. But certainly the girl would never have ridden into battle, never have been willing to die because you were as good as most.

JOAN

(*Comes forward, smiling, happy*)

Oh, Warwick, I wasn't paying any attention to Charlie. I knew what Charlie was like. I wanted him crowned because I wanted my country back. And God gave it to us on this Coronation Day. Let's end with it, please, if nobody would mind.

As the curtain falls the chorus sings the "Gloria" of the Mass.